Obsessive-compulsive disorder

An information guide

Neil A. Rector, PhD
Christina Bartha, MSW
Kate Kitchen, MSW
Martin Katzman, MD
Margaret Richter, MD

Revised by Lakshmi Ravindran, MD, Rosalia Yoon, MSc, PhD and Adele Efendov, PhD, CPsych

Centre for Addiction and Mental Health

A Pan American Health Organization /
World Health Organization Collaborating Centre

Library and Archives Canada Cataloguing in Publication

Rector, Neil A., author
    Obsessive-compulsive disorder: an information guide / Neil A. Rector, PhD, Christina Bartha, MSW, Kate Kitchen, MSW, Martin Katzman, MD, Margaret Richter, MD ; revised by Lakshmi Ravindran, MD, Rosalia Yoon, MSc, PhD and Adele Efendov, PhD, C.Psych. -- Revised edition.

Revision of: Obsessive-compulsive disorder: an information guide. Toronto: Centre for Addiction and Mental Health, 2001.
Includes bibliographical references.
Issued in print and electronic formats.
ISBN 978-1-77114-347-9 (PAPERBACK). -- ISBN 978-1-77114-348-6 (PDF). -- ISBN 978-1-77114-349-3 (HTML). -- ISBN 978-1-77114-350-9 (EPUB). -- ISBN 978-1-77114-351-6 (KINDLE)

    1. Obsessive-compulsive disorder--Popular works. 2. Obsessive-compulsive disorder--Patients--Family relationships. I. Bartha, Christina, author II. Kitchen, Kate, author III. Katzman, Martin A., author IV. Richter, Peggy (Margaret A.), author V. Centre for Addiction and Mental Health, issuing body VI. Title.

RC533.R438 2016   616.85'227   C2016-903236-1
C2016-903237-X

Printed in Canada

Copyright © 2001, 2016 Centre for Addiction and Mental Health

This publication may be available in other formats. For information about alternative formats or other CAMH publications, or to place an order, please contact CAMH Publications:
Toll-free: 1 800 661-1111
Toronto: 416 595-6059
E-mail: publications@camh.ca
Online store: http://store.camh.ca
Website: www.camh.ca

Disponible en français sous le titre :
Le trouble obsessionnel-compulsif : Guide à l'intention des personnes ayant un trouble obsessionel-compulsif et de leur famille

This guide was produced by CAMH Education.

3973a / 08-2016 / PM123

Contents

iv

Acknowledgments

We thank the patients who shared their personal experience with OCD. We also thank those patients and family members who provided anonymous reviews of earlier drafts.

Introduction

This guide is for people with OCD, their families, partners, friends and anyone else who might be interested. This book will answer some common questions about many aspects of OCD and help readers discuss obsessive-compulsive disorder with treatment providers.

1 What is obsessive-compulsive disorder?

I obsess about causing harm to others through some unintentional act. I worry that I have hurt someone with my sloppy or ineffectual words and will cause them to become seriously unhappy. Or that I have left a cigarette burning in my house or an appliance on and that my house will explode and wipe out the whole neighbourhood. This causes me to check things more than once before I leave the house, and then to go back into the house to check again. — Mary W.

Obsessive-compulsive disorder (OCD) is a severe and debilitating mental illness characterized by the presence of obsessions and compulsions. OCD affects about two per cent of the population. It exists throughout the world and it affects women at a slightly higher rate than males in adulthood. Symptoms usually begin gradually and about a quarter of people with OCD start to develop the disorder in early adolescence.

What are obsessions?

Everyone has bothersome worries now and again. We may worry about a problem at work or school, about money, health, relationships or a family member. People with OCD, however, can become consumed by worry. These worries are not like those that people would normally expect to have; they are not worries about real-life problems.

When worries consume someone, we call them "obsessions." Obsessions are uninvited or "intrusive" thoughts, urges or images that surface in the mind over and over again. People with OCD know their obsessions are unrealistic creations of their own minds, but they can't get rid of them, they can't control them, and they can't ignore them. Some of the more common obsessions afflicting people with OCD are:

CONTAMINATION

· fear of contamination by dirt, germs or other diseases (for example, by shaking hands)
· fear of own saliva, urine, feces, semen or vaginal fluids

REPEATED DOUBTING

· fear of having done (or not done) a specific act that could result in harm (for example, hurting someone in a traffic accident, leaving a door unlocked or not turning off the stove)
· fear of having made a mistake

ORDERING

- fear that things will not be "just right," and distress when things are shifted or touched
- focus on exactness and order

RELIGIOUS

- fear of having blasphemous thoughts
- preoccupation with religious images and thoughts

AGGRESSIVE

- fear of harming oneself (for example, while eating with a knife or a fork, handling sharp objects or walking near glass windows)
- fear of harming others (for example, poisoning people's food, harming babies, pushing someone in front of a train or hurting someone's feelings)
- fear of blurting out obscenities in public

SEXUAL

- forbidden or unwanted sexual thoughts, images or urges (for example, experiencing recurrent sexually explicit images)
- being obsessed with sexual thoughts that involve children or incest
- fear of being homosexual

People with OCD may regard their obsessions as unwanted, unacceptable and sometimes disgusting, causing them significant feelings of distress and anxiety. To relieve these feelings, people with OCD often engage in repetitive behaviours, mental acts or rituals.

What are compulsions?

Many people have rituals, or specific ways of doing things. We may read the paper when we wake up in the morning, or arrange pencils and erasers in a particular order on our desk. For people with OCD, such rituals may become "stuck" and last for hours.

Even though the person performing the ritual often knows it makes no sense, he or she feels compelled to enact it over and over again. When taken to this extreme, rituals are called "compulsions." Acting out these compulsions does not give people with OCD pleasure, but it can help them feel less anxious or distressed.

Compulsions can be very rigid and involve elaborate steps. They are either not realistically connected with what they are meant to stop or they are extreme beyond reason. Although this is by no means an exhaustive list, common compulsions include:

CLEANING/WASHING

· washing hands too often or in a ritualized way; showering; bathing; brushing teeth; grooming a lot or having detailed toilet routines; cleaning household items or other objects
· avoiding objects and situations considered "contaminated"

CHECKING

· checking that you don't harm others or yourself; checking that nothing terrible happens; checking that you don't make mistakes

ORDERING/ARRANGING

· making sure things, such as bed sheets or notes on the desk, are "just right," or consistent with a specific rule

MENTAL RITUALS

· mentally repeating special words, images or numbers
· special prayers
· mental reviewing
· mental undoing, or replacing bad thoughts with good thoughts

How does OCD affect people?

The impact of OCD on a person's quality of life is strikingly high. Every aspect of a person's life can be affected, including the way the person thinks, feels or behaves. People with OCD may avoid situations that could trigger symptoms, and because they are often aware that their thoughts and actions are unrealistic, they may have difficulty sharing their concern or seeking help for their problems. The intensity of the symptoms can range from mild to severe, and the symptoms usually wax and wane over time. In severe cases (up to 20 per cent of those with the diagnosis) obsessions and compulsions can occupy the entire day and result in profound disability.

People with OCD often live with the disorder for many years before it is diagnosed and treated. Fortunately, treatment is now widely available and can be very effective in lifting the burden of this demanding and devastating illness.

Diagnosing OCD

Many people have unwanted thoughts, worries and behavioural routines. We may dwell on unpleasant thoughts, worry about our loved ones or bite our nails. An accurate diagnosis of OCD, however must differentiate between these behaviours and the actual psychiatric condition.

The American Psychiatric Association (2013) defines obsessive-compulsive disorder in its diagnostic reference, the *Diagnostic and Statistical Manual of Mental Disorders* (DSM-5), as follows:

> *OCD is characterized by the presence of obsessions and/or compulsions. Obsessions are recurrent and persistent thoughts, urges, or images that are experienced as intrusive and unwanted, whereas compulsions are repetitive behaviors or mental acts that an individual feels driven to perform in response to an obsession or according to rules that must be applied rigidly. . . . These obsessions or compulsions are time-consuming (e.g. take more than 1 hour per day) or cause clinically significant distress or impairment in social, occupational, or other important areas of functioning* (pp. 235–237).

Clinicians are skilled at using psychiatric examinations and questionnaires to determine the seriousness of the obsessions and compulsions, and the extent to which these symptoms cause distress and interfere in the person's day-to-day life. Before making a diagnosis of OCD, however, clinicians are careful to check whether the problems might be better explained by other disorder(s) that have symptoms similar to those of OCD. This process of elimination is called *differential diagnosis*. Below is a list of disorders that may have OCD-like symptoms. Note: While these conditions are different from OCD, many can occur at the same time as OCD.

Conditions with symptoms similar to OCD

OBSESSIVE-COMPULSIVE PERSONALITY DISORDER

Obsessive-compulsive personality disorder (OCPD) is a personality disorder commonly confused with OCD, though the majority of people with OCPD do not have OCD. OCPD is characterized by personality traits reflecting extreme perfectionism, indecision and preoccupation with details and rules. People with OCPD must have things their way with family, friends and colleagues; they may show excessive devotion to work and are often considered workaholics. They may be over-conscientious and show little expression of affection or enjoyment with others, and some people may characterize those with OCPD as "stingy." While most people with OCD may report having one or two of these traits, a diagnosis of OCPD requires that the person have five of these traits, and there are clear and important differences between the two diagnoses.

OBSESSIVE-COMPULSIVE RELATED DISORDERS

Obsessive-compulsive related disorders (OCRDs) is a group of disorders involving repetitive thoughts and/or behaviours that are difficult to ignore or suppress, and that cause significant distress or impairment in social, occupational or other areas of functioning. Although different from OCD, OCRDs are closely related to and often co-occur with OCD. They include:

· **Body dysmorphic disorder:** Characterized by excessive worry about appearance and what are perceived to be physical defects or flaws that are not observable or appear minimal to others. This preoccupation often leads to excessively repetitive behaviours or mental acts, such as mirror checking, grooming, requests for reassurance or seeking cosmetic procedures.

· **Trichotillomania:** Characterized by pulling out hairs from regions in which hair grows (for example, the scalp, eyebrows, eyelids and limbs), resulting in hair loss, despite repeated attempts to decrease or stop. While compulsions in OCD are performed to reduce distress associated with obsessions, in trichotillomania the compulsive behaviour is not aimed at neutralizing obsessions.

· **Excoriation (skin picking) disorder:** Characterized by recurrent skin picking that results in skin lesions, despite repeated attempts to decrease or stop.

· **Hoarding disorder:** Characterized by persistent difficulty in discarding or parting with possessions, regardless of their value. This results in excessive accumulation of possessions that clutter living areas.

> *Things keep coming in to my home but nothing goes out. I don't think I even know what I have because of everything being so mixed up. NO ONE has been in the apartment for years. I'm sure my landlords would throw me out if they saw the condition of my place. I often think, what if there was a fire? I don't dare light candles and I love candles. I'm fearful of meeting someone I could care about because I could never bring him here to my home and he would be as disgusted with me as I am with myself.* — Aubrey D.

TIC DISORDERS

Tics are sudden, rapid motor movements or vocalizations. Similar to trichotillomania, tics are not preceded by obsessions and are not engaged in to reduce obsessional distress. Tic disorders are common in people with OCD, especially when the OCD began in childhood, and some complex tics can be difficult to distinguish from compulsions. However, tic disorders differ from OCD in that tics are not preceded by obsessions, and are not aimed at neutralizing obsessions.

PSYCHOTIC DISORDERS

Psychotic disorders are characterized by the presence of delusions, hallucinations, disorganized thinking and disorganized or abnormal motor behaviour. Although some individuals with ocd have poor insight or even delusional beliefs that may appear to stem from a psychotic disorder such as schizophrenia, ocd differs from psychotic disorders in that levels of insight can change with severity of ocd. Moreover, other symptoms of psychotic disorders—such as auditory and visual hallucinations, and difficulties with speech—are not commonly observed in people with ocd.

DEPRESSION

People with depression often ruminate about past mistakes and perceived failures, which may be confused with obsessions. However, unlike people with ocd—who experience distress and the urge to neutralize and/or avoid recurring thoughts or images—people with depression often brood over their depressed state to better understand its causes and consequences. Moreover, depression is usually accompanied by other symptoms that are not present in ocd, such as loss of interest in activities, fatigue, and appetite and weight changes.

ANXIETY DISORDERS

People with ocd often experience symptoms of anxiety and, conversely, people with anxiety disorders can experience symptoms of ocd, such as recurrent thoughts and avoidant behaviours. However, the two disorders differ in that worries in anxiety disorders are normally about real-life concerns, and are not accompanied by compulsions.

Common anxiety disorders include:

- **Generalized anxiety disorder:** Characterized by excessive anxiety or worry about real-life concerns, such as finances or health.
- **Panic disorder:** Characterized by recurring panic attacks, which may occur with or without agoraphobia (fear of leaving secure places).
- **Social phobia:** Fear of embarrassment or humiliation in social situations.
- **Specific phobia:** Fear of a particular object or situation, such as spiders or heights.
- **Post-traumatic stress disorder:** Fear and anxiety re-experienced in flashbacks of traumatic events.

2 What causes OCD?

As far back as I can remember, my family and friends referred to me as a worrywart. When I was about the age of 16, my experiences with OCD began. I had just started high school and things were stressful with all the changes. A friend of mine had been afflicted with a case of food poisoning, and that was when I acquired my fear of being poisoned. I can still remember how it started as a tiny concern, and proceeded to snowball into the major preoccupation of my life. — Cecilia D.

Despite considerable research into the possible causes of OCD, no clear answer has emerged. As with most psychiatric conditions, different factors may be involved. At present, the most we can say is that OCD appears to be caused by a combination of psychological and biological factors. We will explore the theories in this chapter and the related treatments in Chapters 3 and 4.

Psychological factors

Many psychological theories have been introduced to explain the development of OCD. The two that have received the greatest support are the behavioural and cognitive theories.

BEHAVIOURAL THEORY

The behavioural theory suggests that people with ocd associate certain objects or situations with fear, and learn to avoid the things they fear or to perform rituals that help reduce the fear.

This pattern of fear and avoidance or ritual may begin when people are under periods of high emotional stress, such as starting a new job or ending a relationship. At such times, we are more vulnerable to fear and anxiety. Often things once regarded as "neutral" may begin to bring on feelings of fear. For example, a person who has always been able to use public toilets may, when under stress, make a connection between the toilet seat and a fear of catching an illness.

Once a connection between an object and the feeling of fear becomes established, people with ocd avoid the things they fear, rather than confronting or tolerating the fear. For instance, the person who fears catching an illness from public toilets will avoid using them. When forced to use a public toilet, he or she will perform elaborate cleaning rituals, such as cleaning the toilet seat, cleaning the door handles of the cubicle or following a detailed washing procedure. Because these actions temporarily reduce the level of fear, the fear is never challenged and dealt with and the behaviour is reinforced. The association of fear may spread to other objects, such as public sinks and showers.

In behavioural therapy (discussed in detail in the next chapter), people with ocd learn to confront and reduce their anxiety without practising avoidance or ritual behaviour. When they learn to directly confront their fears, they become less afraid.

COGNITIVE THEORY

While the behavioural theory focuses on how people with OCD make an association between an object and fear, the cognitive theory focuses on how people with OCD misinterpret their thoughts.

Most people have intrusive or uninvited thoughts similar to those reported by people with OCD. For example, parents under stress from caring for an infant may have an intrusive thought of harming the infant. Most people would be able to shrug off such a thought. Individuals prone to developing OCD, however, might exaggerate the importance of the thought, and respond as though it represents an actual threat. They may think, "I must be a danger to children if I have thoughts of harming children." This can cause a high level of anxiety and other negative emotions, such as shame, guilt and self-disgust.

People who come to fear their own thoughts usually attempt to neutralize feelings that arise from their thoughts. One way they do this is by avoiding situations that might spark such thoughts. Another is by engaging in rituals, such as washing or praying.

Cognitive theory suggests that as long as people interpret intrusive thoughts as catastrophic, and as long as they continue to believe that such thinking holds truth, they will continue to be distressed and to practise avoidance and/or ritual behaviours.

According to cognitive theory, people who attach exaggerated danger to their thoughts do so because of false beliefs learned earlier in life. Researchers think the following beliefs may be important in the development and maintenance of obsessions:
- "exaggerated responsibility," or the belief that one is responsible for preventing misfortunes or harm to others

· the belief that certain thoughts are very important and should be controlled
· the belief that somehow having a thought or an urge to do something will increase the chances that it will come true
· the tendency to overestimate the likelihood of danger
· the belief that one should always be perfect and that mistakes are unacceptable.

> *When I first experienced my* OCD, *I thought I was losing my mind. I had never worried about these ideas before and now I was totally enveloped with them. I knew what I was feeling was unreasonable but I still had this terrifying feeling of "what if?" What if it was at all possible for these things to happen? I knew that the odds were .0001 per cent but I would still be overwhelmed with the fear that something disastrous might occur to me or someone else.*
> — Bryan B.

In cognitive therapy (discussed in detail in the next chapter), people "unlearn" their mistaken beliefs and change their patterns of thought. By doing so, they are able to eliminate the distress associated with such thoughts and to discontinue their compulsive behaviours.

Biological factors

REGULATING BRAIN CHEMISTRY

Research into the biological causes and effects of OCD has revealed a link between OCD and certain brain chemicals, or neurotransmitters. The neurotransmitters that are particularly important in OCD include serotonin, dopamine and glutamate.

Serotonin is one of the brain's chemical messengers that transmits signals between brain cells. Serotonin plays a role in the regulation of mood, aggression, impulse control, sleep, appetite, body temperature and pain. All of the medicines used to treat OCD raise the levels of serotonin available to transmit messages. The roles of dopamine and glutamate are being further researched.

CHANGES IN BRAIN ACTIVITY

Modern brain imaging techniques have allowed researchers to study the activity of specific areas of the brain. Such studies have shown that people with OCD have more than usual activity in three areas of the brain. These are:

- the **caudate nucleus** (specific brain cells in the basal ganglia, deep in the centre of the brain). This area of the brain acts as a filter for thoughts coming in from other areas. The caudate nucleus is also considered to be important in managing habitual and repetitive behaviours. When OCD is successfully treated with drugs or therapy, the activity in this area of the brain usually decreases. This shows that both drugs and psychotherapy can alter the physical functioning of the brain.
- the **prefrontal orbital cortex** (in the front area of the brain). The level of activity in the prefrontal orbital cortex is believed to affect appropriate social behaviour. Lowered activity or damage in this region is linked to feeling uninhibited, poor judgment and a lack of guilt. More activity may therefore cause more worry about social concerns, such as being meticulous, neat and preoccupied with cleanliness, and being afraid of acting inappropriately. All of these concerns are symptoms of OCD.
- the **cingulate gyrus** (in the centre of the brain). The cingulate gyrus is believed to be involved in detecting potential errors as well as contributing to the emotional response to obsessive thoughts. Essentially, this area of the brain tells you that you have made a

mistake and to perform a behaviour to correct it. This region is highly interconnected with the prefrontal orbital cortex and the basal ganglia, via a number of brain cell pathways.

The basal ganglia, the prefrontal orbital cortex and the cingulate gyrus all have many brain cells affected by serotonin. Researchers believe that medicines that raise the levels of serotonin available to transmit messages may change the level of activity in these areas of the brain.

STREPTOCOCCUS AND OCD

Some researchers believe that cases in which children suddenly develop ocd or Tourette's syndrome may be linked to a recent infection with Group A streptococcus, the bacteria that causes the common strep throat. In these cases, the body may be forming antibodies to the infection, which may mistakenly react to the basal ganglia, an area of the brain linked to ocd.

There is no evidence, however, that streptococcus plays a role in adult-onset ocd. And in most cases where children develop ocd, the symptoms begin gradually, not suddenly as described above. At this time, then, the link between streptococcus infection and ocd is not certain.

GENETIC FACTORS

OCD often seems to run in families. In fact, almost half of all cases show a familial pattern. Research studies on families of people with ocd, as well as data from national health registries, indicate that first-, second- and third-degree relatives of people with ocd have a greater chance of developing ocd than does someone with no family history of the disorder.

When a medical disorder runs in families, it can be due either to genes that are passed on (hereditary) or to shared environment ("taught" by one family member to another). In OCD, it is believed that genetic factors play an important role in the tendency to develop obsessions and compulsions. Evidence for this belief comes from twin studies, which show that if one twin has OCD, the other twin is far more likely to develop the disorder if they are identical twins (who share 100 per cent of genetic material) than if they are fraternal twins (who share about 50 per cent of genetic material).

Research studies on the genetics of OCD indicate that there is no one gene specifically linked to OCD. Rather, it appears that multiple combinations of different genes can contribute to the total risk of developing OCD. These include variants of genes that regulate neurotransmitters such as serotonin, dopamine and glutamate. However, much of the genetic contribution to OCD remains unknown.

3 Therapy for OCD

Modern treatments for OCD have radically changed how the disorder is viewed. While in the past OCD was regarded as chronic and untreatable, a diagnosis of OCD may now be regarded with hope. Cognitive-behavioural therapy (CBT) and antidepressant medications are currently used to treat the disorder. Neither provide a cure for OCD, but they control the symptoms and enable people with OCD to restore normal function in their lives.

Treatment for OCD ideally involves a combination of CBT and drug therapy. It is important that people with OCD receive treatment that is specific to OCD, from a fully qualified therapist. Some forms of traditional psychotherapy are not effective at relieving symptoms of OCD. CBT is often delivered in a group setting because there are benefits in meeting and working with people who have the same difficulties.

Many people with OCD benefit from supportive counselling in addition to treatments aimed at reducing the symptoms of OCD. Individuals may see a therapist one-on-one, or counselling may also involve the partner, spouse or family. For more information on supportive counselling, see Chapter 5.

Cognitive-behavioural therapy

Cognitive-behavioural therapy (CBT) refers to two distinct treatments: cognitive therapy and behavioural therapy. The most widely practised behavioural therapy for OCD is called exposure and response prevention (ERP).

Although these treatments are increasingly offered in combination, we will discuss them separately.

EXPOSURE AND RESPONSE PREVENTION

The "exposure" part of this treatment involves direct or imagined controlled exposure to objects or situations that trigger obsessions that arouse anxiety. Over time, exposure to these obsessional cues leads to less and less anxiety and eventually arouses little anxiety at all. This process of getting used to obsessional cues is called "habituation."

The "response" in part refers to the ritual behaviours that people with OCD engage in to reduce anxiety. In ERP treatment, patients learn to resist the compulsion to perform rituals and are eventually able to stop engaging in these behaviours.

How does ERP work?

Before starting ERP treatment, patients make a list or "hierarchy" of situations that provoke obsessional fears. For example, a person with fears of contamination might create a list of obsessional cues that looks like this:

1) touching garbage   2) using the toilet   3) shaking hands

Treatment starts with exposure to situations that cause mild to moderate anxiety, and as the patient habituates to these situations, he or she gradually works up to situations that cause greater anxiety. The time it takes to progress in treatment depends on the patient's ability to tolerate anxiety and to resist compulsive behaviours.

Exposure tasks are usually first performed with the therapist assisting. These sessions generally take between 45 minutes and three hours. Patients are also asked to practise exposure tasks between sessions for two to three hours per day.

In some cases, direct or "in vivo" exposure to the obsessional fears is not possible in the therapist's office. If, for example, a patient were being treated for an obsession about causing an accident while driving, the therapist would have to practise what is called "imaginal" exposure. Imaginal exposure involves exposing the person to situations that trigger obsessions by imagining different scenes.

The main goal during both in vivo and imaginal exposure is for the person to stay in contact with the obsessional trigger without engaging in ritual behaviours. For example, if the person who fears contamination responds to the anxiety by engaging in hand-washing or cleaning rituals, he or she would be required to resist these activities after an exposure task—first for hours and eventually for days. The therapy continues in this manner until the patient is able to abstain from ritual activities altogether.

To track progress during exposure tasks, patients are trained to be experts in rating their own anxiety levels. Once they have made progress in treatment, participants are encouraged to continue using the ERP techniques they have learned, and to apply them to new situations as they arise. A typical course of ERP treatment is between 14 and 16 weeks.

Self-directed ERP

For people with mild OCD, self-directed ERP may be as effective as seeing a therapist. Two excellent self-directed ERP manuals with step-by-step strategies are *Getting Control* and *Stop Obsessing!"* (See "Suggested Reading" on page 53.)

How effective is ERP?

Even patients with long-standing and severe symptoms of OCD can benefit from ERP treatment. Success depends on a number of factors and requires that the patient be motivated to get well.

Studies documenting the benefits of ERP treatment have found that upwards of 75 per cent of patients experience improvement in their OCD symptoms during treatment. The majority show long-term improvement two and three years after treatment.

Patients who benefit less from ERP include those who do not exhibit overt compulsions and those with moderate-to-severe depression.

COGNITIVE THERAPY

As mentioned earlier, people with OCD often become anxious about their thoughts (or obsessions) when they interpret such thoughts as dangerous and likely to occur. Thoughts of leaving the house with the stove on, for example, can result in a debilitating anxiety that sends the person running back to check again and again.

How does cognitive therapy work?

In the treatment of OCD, cognitive therapy is most often done in combination with ERP.

Patients create a hierarchy of situations that cause distress and when they participate in exposure tasks, they are asked to pay particular attention to thoughts and feelings related to these situations.

In cognitive therapy, the focus is on how participants interpret their obsessions: what they believe or assume to be true about them, what their attitude is toward them and why they think they have these obsessions. For example, a person who fears shaking hands may believe it will pass on germs that may cause him to become ill. This interpretation of this fear can be challenged and re-interpreted so that he no longer views shaking hands as a high-risk activity. Achieving these results takes time, but can provide effective relief.

Cognitive therapy also helps participants identify and re-evaluate beliefs about the potential consequences of engaging or not engaging in compulsive behaviour, and work toward eliminating this behaviour. For example, someone who compulsively washes her hands for 30 minutes at a time may believe that she is doing so to guard against infection. When this belief is challenged and confronted as false, it can help to control the behaviour.

One tool used in cognitive therapy to help people identify, challenge and correct negative interpretations of intrusive thoughts is the thought record. In the thought record, participants record their obsessions and their interpretations associated with the obsessions. The first step is for the person to begin to record each and every time they experience an intrusive thought, image or idea. The important details to record include:

1. Where was I when the obsession began?
2. What intrusive thought/image/idea did I have?
3. What meaning did I apply to having the intrusive thought/image/idea?
4. What did I do?

An example of a thought record

SITUATION: Sitting at home watching television.

INTRUSIVE THOUGHT: "God doesn't care."

APPRAISAL OF INTRUSIVE THOUGHT:
1. I am a bad person for thinking blasphemous thoughts.
2. God will punish my family and me.
3. I must be losing my mind if I can't stop these thoughts from happening.

RITUAL: Engage in prayer. Engage in behaviours of atonement.

After the person learns to identify intrusive thoughts and the meanings they apply to them, the next steps are:
· Examine the evidence that supports and does not support the obsession.
· Identify cognitive distortions in the appraisals of the obsession.
· Begin to develop a less threatening and alternative response to the intrusive thought/image/idea.

These patterns are identified in session together with the therapist, and again during actual exposure exercises. Then the person continues to record information on the thought record between sessions.

How effective is cognitive therapy?

Studies have shown that cognitive therapy is an effective treatment for OCD. Although cognitive and behavioural therapy can be separate, many therapists combine the two strategies. Patients can benefit from both cognitive restructuring and exposure exercises.

> *My experience in group therapy has been extremely beneficial, as I have gained much greater insight into my disorder and have been given many useful tools by*

my therapists to help me to learn to live with OCD. Although the weekly homework was particularly difficult for me, being a list maker and a checker, it afforded me plenty of practice learning to alleviate the anxiety that it caused. Meeting other people who suffer from OCD has allowed me to experience a shared empathy, which has helped me shift my focus outside of myself. Their understanding and support has made my struggle far less lonely and hopeless.

Thanks to the strategies learned in the group I now know I can have control over my OCD. Although at first it was very difficult to confront my fears, doing this has paid great dividends in the reduction of my symptoms. Working through my OCD challenges with others in the group has made me feel that I am by no means alone or unusual in this struggle. Listening to the challenges and triumphs of the other group members has motivated me to challenge myself more and continue to loosen the grip OCD has had on my life.
— Changying X.

4 Medications

If left untreated, ocd can be a disabling and chronic illness. In addition to cognitive-behavioural therapy, drug therapy can help to reduce symptoms of ocd.

As outlined in the section "Regulating Brain Chemistry" (page 14), research has shown that people with ocd often benefit from drugs that increase the levels of serotonin available to transmit messages in the brain.

The main medications that do this are known as serotonin reuptake inhibitors (sris). They are the most commonly prescribed drugs in the treatment of ocd, and are also used to treat depression. sris belong to a class of drugs called antidepressants.

Most doctors treating ocd with medication will prescribe an sri. This medication helps to reduce the symptoms of ocd for a majority of the people who take it. For those who do not benefit from taking sri drugs, other drug treatments may provide relief. Other drugs may also be prescribed to address specific symptoms, and taken in addition to sris. This chapter gives an overview of drug therapy options, including discussion of side-effects and other concerns.

Serotonin reuptake inhibitors

There are two types of serotonin reuptake inhibitors (SRIS). The newer kinds are known as *selective* serotonin reuptake inhibitors (SSRIS) because their primary effect is on serotonin neurotransmitters. The SSRIS currently available in Canada are fluoxetine (Prozac), fluvoxamine (Luvox), sertraline (Zoloft), paroxetine (Paxil), citalopram (Celexa) and escitalopram (Cipralex). These medications are considered to be equally effective, although some may work for certain people but not for others.

Clomipramine (Anafranil) is the oldest and best studied of the SRI medications. It belongs to a class of medications called tricyclic antidepressants. Research indicates that clomipramine may be slightly more effective for OCD than the SSRIS, with about 80 per cent of people who take it reporting a reduction in symptoms. However, clomipramine has a more complicated set of side-effects than the SSRIS. While all SRIS are effective, most doctors advise patients with OCD to try one of the SSRIS first, because they generally have more tolerable side-effects.

WHAT'S INVOLVED IN TRYING SRIs?

For best results, SRIS should be taken regularly, generally once each day. Most doctors recommend starting at a low dose and then, if the patient tolerates the medication well, slowly increasing the dose. People who take SRIS may experience side-effects, so the ideal dose is one that provides the greatest benefit with a minimum of side-effects.

For people with OCD, the response to medication may take longer than for depression or anxiety disorders—sometimes between eight and 12 weeks. That is why a person who has begun to take an SRI should continue for at least three months. This allows time for the dosage to be adjusted correctly and for the benefits of the drug to become clear. When these drugs work, the effects come on gradually. Usually several weeks pass before any change in symptoms is noticed, although some individuals may see a more rapid improvement.

Typically, obsessions and compulsions slowly become less intense. It is important to realize that although these medications can be of great help to some people, only rarely do they provide relief from all symptoms of OCD.

If no benefits are derived from a particular SRI medication after a trial period of three months, doctors often recommend that another SRI be tried. Some individuals respond well to one drug and not at all to another. If a person does not benefit from the first medication, a second choice may be clomipramine.

It is not uncommon for someone to try two or three SRI drugs before finding the one that works best. People usually try at least three drugs in the SRI class before considering other drugs.

The question of whether or not to take SRIs while pregnant or nursing should be discussed with your doctor. In some cases, the benefit of the drug clearly outweighs the possible risks.

HOW LONG SHOULD I TAKE AN SRI?

When the right SRI drug has been found, doctors usually advise taking the medication for at least six to 12 months. In some cases, it may be best to take the medication for the long term, as there may be a high risk of relapse if the medication is stopped. Even when taken long term, these medications are not addictive.

If the person begins to feel better and stops taking the medication too soon or too abruptly, the risk of relapse increases. The decision to stop taking medication should only be made in consultation with a doctor. These guidelines can help to lower the risk of relapse when a person stops using medication:

· Lower the dosage gradually by tapering or reducing the medication over time, possibly several months.
· Follow up with a health care professional regularly to help monitor the severity of any symptoms of OCD.
· Combine cognitive-behavioural therapy with medication and use the skills learned to control any symptoms that may arise when medication is discontinued.

SIDE-EFFECTS OF SRIs

People who take SRIS may experience side-effects. For some, the side-effects are mild, an easy trade-off for the benefits of the medication. For others, the side-effects may be more troubling. People often experience the side-effects of SRIs before they experience the benefits.

In general, the side-effects of SRIs diminish over time, allowing people to tolerate these medications quite well over the long term. Some side-effects may be reduced by adjusting the dose or by taking the dose at a different time of day. The side-effects of SRIs have no permanent effect and will disappear completely when the medication is discontinued. When taking SRIs or any medication, it is important to discuss any side-effects that are troubling you with your doctor.

The possible side-effects of the newer SSRIs are generally considered to be more manageable than those of the older SRI, clomipramine. Many of the common side-effects of the newer and older drugs are the same. They include dry mouth, sweating, constipation, drowsiness, tremor and sexual side-effects, such as lower sex drive, delayed orgasm or inability to have an orgasm.

Weight gain is considered to be more of an issue with clomipramine, although it can also occur with long-term use of ssris.

Other common possible side-effects of ssris are nausea, sleeplessness and headaches.

Other common possible side-effects of clomipramine are dizziness with sudden changes in posture, and blurred vision. Possible, but rare, side-effects are manic episodes and seizures. Individuals with a history of certain heart problems should use clomipramine with caution, as this drug affects how electrical impulses are conducted through the heart.

DRUG INTERACTIONS WITH SRIs

When taking sris, or any medication, it is important to check with a doctor or pharmacist for possible drug interactions before taking any other prescription or over-the-counter drugs.

Generally, sris are safe drugs to use. However, taking the antihistamines terfenadine (Seldane) and astemizole (Hismanal) while taking sris can be dangerous. Other types of antihistamines are safe. sris are also known to interfere with the effectiveness of some commonly prescribed drugs.

When taking sris, it may be wise to avoid alcohol. sris may intensify the effect of alcohol, making it more difficult to control how alcohol affects your behaviour. Alcohol may also interfere with the effectiveness of sris.

Other medications

For those who try several SRIS without benefit, there are other medications that may help. In some cases, other types of antidepressants may be helpful. In others, a second drug is given in addition to an SRI.

OTHER ANTIDEPRESSANTS

These drugs also affect the brain chemical serotonin, but they work differently from the SRIS.

Serotonin-norepinephrine reuptake inhibitors

This class of antidepressants (SNRIS for short) also works on norepinephrine and can be quite tolerable. Medications in this group include venlafaxine (Effexor), desvenlafaxine (Pristiq) and duloxetine (Cymbalta). However, we have less information about their effectiveness for OCD, so if they are used, it may be as a second or third choice.

Monoamine oxidase inhibitors

Monoamine oxidase inhibitors (MAOIS) are effective antidepressants and are known to have some limited benefits in OCD. The two MAOIS available are phenelzine (Nardil) and tranylcipramine (Parnate). Both are less effective against obsessions than are SRIS, and both have more complicated side-effects than SRIS, as well as requiring a special diet, so they are typically used only if SRI medications fail.

Secondary medications

In some cases, a second medication in combination with an SRI can be very helpful in treating the symptoms of OCD. Adding a second drug to a primary drug is known as augmentation.

DRUGS TO RELIEVE ANXIETY

Antipsychotics

There is growing evidence that combining antipsychotic medication with an antidepressant may further reduce symptoms of OCD. As a result, it is becoming more common to add a medication from this class for people who have had only a partial response to an antidepressant. There are two types of antipsychotics: the older "typical" and the newer "atypical" antipsychotics.

Typical antipsychotics, such as haloperidol (Haldol), may be especially helpful in relieving symptoms for people who have both OCD and tic disorder or Tourette's syndrome. There are also several atypical antipsychotics available in Canada, including risperidone (Risperdal), olanzapine (Zyprexa), quetiapine (Seroquel) and aripiprazole (Abilify). Risperidone currently has the best evidence for effectiveness in treating OCD, although the others are also frequently used.

Unfortunately, these drugs are not without risk or side-effects. Antipsychotics can be quite sedating, and so hard to tolerate. They also carry longer-term risk, particularly the atypical drugs. Specifically, there are metabolic risks, including increased appetite, weight gain, elevated triglyceride and cholesterol levels, and diabetes. These risks mean that regular monitoring and blood work is important. Although it is less common with the newer drugs, some people who take antipsychotic medication for a long time may develop involuntary movements, a condition known as tardive dyskinesia. For every year that a person receives antipsychotic medication, there is a five per cent chance of developing tardive dyskinesia. The effects cannot always be reversed.

Benzodiazepines

These medications have a calming effect and can help to reduce anxiety and make it easier to get to sleep. But it is not clear whether they reduce the intensity of obsessions or compulsions. People trying to improve their symptoms through cognitive-behavioural therapy should avoid benzodiazepine drugs, because they may affect short-term memory and learning.

While these drugs can help to reduce anxiety, they should be used with caution. When starting one of these drugs, avoid driving or operating machinery until you are used to the effect. Also avoid using alcohol while taking benzodiazepines, because this combination can be dangerous. Long-term use of benzodiazepines may lead to dependence in some people. Withdrawal from these drugs should be monitored by a doctor.

Of these medications, clonazepam (Rivotril) may specifically affect serotonin balance and is a good choice for people with ocd. Other alternatives that are commonly prescribed include lorazepam (Ativan), alprazolam (Xanax), diazepam (Valium), oxazepam (Serax) and temazepam (Restoril).

Herbal treatments

Certain herbs may have some benefit in reducing symptoms of ocd, but their effectiveness has not yet been tested. For a couple of reasons, people who wish to explore alternative treatments should consult with a knowledgeable doctor:
· As with all medications, herbal treatments can have unwanted side-effects and may interact with prescription or over-the-counter medications or other botanicals.
· In North America, the herbal industry is unregulated, meaning that the quality and effectiveness of herbal products is not consistent.

HERBAL TREATMENTS WITH SEDATING EFFECTS

The sedating effects of some herbal medicines are believed to reduce symptoms of anxiety. These plants include German chamomile, hops, kava, lemon balm, passion flower, skullcap, valerian and gota cola. Compounds in these traditional medicines are known to act on systems in the brain in a similar way to the benzodiazepine class of medications.

Although these plants appear to be safe, they should be used with caution, because they can increase the sedating effects of other medications, as well as alcohol.

HERBAL TREATMENTS WITHOUT SEDATING EFFECTS

St. John's wort has been suggested as a treatment for mild to moderate depression, though recent research suggests that it is actually ineffective for treatment of OCD.

Other herbs, such as Ginkgo biloba and evening primrose oil, have also been suggested for the treatment of OCD, also with little evidence for their effectiveness.

5 Recovery and relapse prevention

The process of recovery

While cognitive-behavioural therapy and medication usually help to reduce the symptoms of OCD, there are aspects of living with the illness that these therapies do not fully address. The process of recovery from OCD, like the onset of the illness, is gradual and ongoing.

OCD affects every part of a person's life. It may disrupt your ability to function at work, in social situations and in the family. Once the symptoms improve and you approach a return to normal life, it can be difficult to address the practical and emotional issues that may have arisen out of a long illness.

A lengthy illness can lower a person's self-confidence, making him or her feel insecure and vulnerable in situations that were once familiar and comfortable. OCD can cause people to become quite dependent on those around them. People are often surprised at how frightened they are at the prospect of being independent and resuming their responsibilities. These reactions are a normal part of the recovery phase of OCD.

Recovery is a process, not a discrete event. At first, you should ease into familiar activities with modest expectations. Slowly take on responsibilities and build your self-confidence. When you return to activities such as socializing and going to school or work, you will probably feel anxious. Allow yourself to make mistakes.

RETURNING TO WORK

The support of a therapist can be helpful in dealing with a return to work or school, and in rebuilding relationships with family and friends. For example, you may feel quite anxious about returning to your job. Some of the work-related issues often raised by people with ocd are:

· How do I explain my absence to co-workers?
· Is it normal to feel insecure and struggle with a lack of confidence?
· How do I understand and manage these feelings and issues without needing to engage in compulsive behaviours?

You may have more, or different, questions about returning to work. Once you have raised your concerns with your therapist, work together on a strategy for a successful return to work.

Ideally, your therapist should be knowledgeable about ocd. Many mental health professionals are not as informed about ocd as they are about other disorders. If a knowledgeable therapist is not available in your community, one who is open to learning about the disorder can give you the support you need.

It is best to resume your responsibilities gradually. Do this by starting back to work part-time or with a reduced workload. Your health care provider may recommend specific job accommodations that could be helpful in this transition, such as more frequent breaks, time off to attend medical appointments and a reduction in non-essential job duties.

It may be helpful to educate your employer and co-workers about some of the typical signs of ocd, though some people prefer not to discuss their illness with employers. If you remain private about your illness, you will not be able to ask for any job accommodations, but it does not mean your transition back to work won't succeed. It can be especially important in this situation to have people outside of work with whom you can discuss your problems and concerns.

Effective relapse prevention

OCD, like physical illnesses such as diabetes, is a chronic condition. Although the symptoms can be reduced and controlled with medication and therapy, you need to take precautions to prevent the symptoms from returning.

It is important to be aware of how you are feeling. Anxiety, stress, fatigue and feeling out of control can trigger a relapse. For some people, certain situations or conditions can trigger symptoms. Another common cause of relapse is stopping medication too soon or too fast.

Once the symptoms of ocd have improved, a number of strategies can help to maintain the gains you have made.

I.   **Become knowledgeable about ocd.**

Read as much as you can about ocd and its treatment. See the list of recommended reading and websites on page 53. If there is something you do not understand, ask your mental health care providers.

2. **Resist compulsive urges; learn and use healthy strategies for coping with stress and fears.**

    Once the symptoms of ocd have improved, maintaining these gains requires commitment and determination. Unhealthy strategies for coping with stress and fears must be replaced with healthy ones. Resist the urge to perform compulsions.

    Using skills learned in therapy, continue to work to eliminate obsessive patterns of thought and compulsive behaviours. Do not be satisfied with only partial improvement of symptoms. This leaves you vulnerable to relapse.

3. **If medication has been prescribed, continue to take it until your doctor advises you otherwise.**

    When patients begin to feel better, they often stop taking medication. Relapse is more likely if you stop taking your medication too soon. Doctors usually recommend that medication be taken for six months to a year. In some cases, antidepressants may be recommended for several years. If you are experiencing side-effects, you may be tempted to stop taking your medication. It is particularly important not to stop your medication abruptly.

    Rather than making decisions on your own, work with your doctor to develop a treatment plan you can live with.

4. **Involve some family and friends in your recovery.**

    If you allow yourself to become isolated and keep your inner world a secret, you will create an ideal breeding ground for symptoms of ocd. When family and friends are aware and involved in your struggle, they can help in a number of ways. For example, they can help you control compulsive urges, help you guard against a recurrence of symptoms and give you support and encouragement.

Who you tell about your illness is a very personal choice. As a buffer against relapse, however, have at least one person you can rely on and confide in.

Along with family, friends and professional support, many people struggling with ocd find that self-help and support groups are a valuable part of their social network. (See the Internet resources on page 53 for information on how to find out if there is an ocd group in your community.)

5. **Adopt a healthy lifestyle that includes proper nutrition, exercise and good sleep habits.**

Your eating, sleeping and exercise habits play a role in how you feel and in your ability to handle stress. Nourishing yourself physically, emotionally and spiritually helps you to feel alert, calm and able to deal with problems as they arise. Yoga, other movement therapies and meditation reduce anxiety. They can also increase energy, concentration and a feeling of well-being.

6. **Try to develop a well-balanced life with enough time for work, family, friends and leisure activities.**

It might seem easy at first to escape from ocd by focusing entirely on one area, such as work or a hobby. Eventually, though, this coping strategy may not work and you will need to develop other aspects of your life. It is important to keep in contact with all the facets of life, such as school, work or volunteer activities, family and friends, and hobbies. As you recover, investing energy into several areas will help you to develop a more balanced and satisfying lifestyle, which will help you to avoid relapse.

7.   **Get follow-up treatment.**

Continuing with treatment, even when the symptoms have
improved, can help maintain the gains and prevent a relapse. Depending on your needs, you may also benefit from
individual, group or family therapy, or a support group.

8.   **Plan for your time and your future.**

The struggle with OCD can eat up your time and distract you
from thinking about your future. When the symptoms improve, it can be difficult to know what to do with the time that
is suddenly available to you. The possibilities can seem endless
and perhaps overwhelming.

Building a life that is not absorbed by OCD depends on engaging in activities that matter to you and that will help you
to maintain the gains you've made. Some people may be able
to pick up where they left off, and return to work, studies or
other interests that were set aside by the illness. For others,
the choice may be more difficult. In some cases, seeking the
services of an occupational therapist or career counsellor can
help you to narrow the possibilities and make choices that
let you look forward to the days to come.

9.   **Prepare for setbacks.**

If you continue to practise the skills learned in therapy and
follow the tips in the points above, OCD will probably not
gain control of your thoughts and actions again. However,
with OCD, the possibility of relapse is always there. If you
feel as though OCD is beginning to take over your life again,
take action.

Have a plan for early intervention. Consult with your doctor or therapist. An adjustment in medication, or revisiting some of the behavioural strategies learned in therapy, can avert a full relapse.

Relationship with a partner or spouse

OCD can affect your relationship with a partner or spouse. During the stage of the illness when symptoms are moderate or severe, it may be hard to be supportive and intimate with your partner.

Over time, this can lead to distance and even hostility in the relationship. It takes time and work to rebuild what might have been lost during the worst stages of the illness, and while the affected person was in treatment.

Couples therapy with a therapist who knows about ocd can be very helpful. A therapist open to learning about ocd can also be effective. You may need someone to help you talk about the problems in the relationship constructively, rather than angrily. A good therapist can open up communication and help couples rediscover what brought them together in the first place. ocd is an illness that must be managed over a person's lifetime. It affects people's activities and goals. Couples may need to grieve the loss of what they imagined their relationship would be like. They may need a new vision of how they will move forward together.

Relationship with children

At its worst, OCD can really affect your personal relationships. It might affect your ability to act as a parent. Routine things such as changing diapers, preparing meals or spending time with your children might become very difficult. You may become isolated from your children's social network and will need to reconnect to school staff, extracurricular activities and neighbours. What, if anything, do you say to people? Your role as parent can be difficult to readjust to when you are recovering from an illness. Talking with a therapist can help you to manage any anxiety that may arise.

6 Help for partners and families

In Mary's family, Mary's OCD became the uncomfortable centrepiece of family life. Mary's fear of contamination led her to wash her family's clothes over and over again. If she didn't, she feared they would become ill and it would be her fault. As Mary's OCD symptoms worsened, she was so afraid of causing the family harm by touching their clothes that she was no longer able to wash their clothes herself. Her husband took over this chore, performing it under Mary's careful supervision. Sometimes someone in the family would become angry and confront Mary over what she agreed were irrational fears, but she was powerless to change. When Mary's OCD was at its worst, she felt that none of her family's clothes were cleaned sufficiently to be worn safely, and she would not allow any of them to leave the house.

What happens when someone you love has OCD?

When someone in a family is ill, everyone is affected, not just the person with the illness. This is true whether the illness is diabetes or OCD. A mental illness brings added pressures. Fearing prejudice, families can become isolated as they struggle to make sense of the diagnosis and treatments.

The symptoms of OCD may not be diagnosed for a long time. Many of the thought patterns and behaviours of OCD are common among the general population, but are within normal limits. If a person complains that their spouse cleans too much or that their son hoards newspapers, people may not take them seriously. A common response might be, "I wish my partner would clean around the house more often" or "Why complain if your son saves newspapers? Is it really any of your business?" When untreated, the symptoms of OCD interfere with normal family life, often to a great degree. It is not unusual for a family to suffer for years before these symptoms are finally diagnosed.

Once an accurate diagnosis is made, getting effective treatment can be difficult. Your community may have few professionals experienced in treating the disorder and no groups available to provide support. Even when the appropriate treatment is found, sometimes people with OCD are reluctant to be treated. They may also reject attempts the family makes to work together to manage the illness.

It's natural for families to feel resentful or disappointed when OCD interferes with normal family life. Acknowledging the illness can be the first step toward feeling less isolated and freeing your energy for caring for both your relative and yourself.

How families are affected by OCD

People with OCD often try to involve family members in compulsive rituals. To keep the peace, family members may play along or help out with behaviours such as hoarding, checking and washing. When a family helps their relative in this way, they are "accommodating" OCD. For example, in one family a wife may buy extra detergent so her husband can wash clothes over and over again. In another, family members may agree not to throw away the piles of newspapers filling the living room.

Accommodating often begins with small compromises. Once it starts, it can be difficult to stop. For example, if a mother's fear of contamination makes grocery shopping an ordeal, her son may go to the grocery store for her. At first, the son does the shopping as an occasional favour, but as his mother's symptoms worsen, he takes it on as a regular chore. Eventually, he does all the shopping. His mother stays home, never leaves the house and becomes completely isolated.

Another way families respond to OCD is with disbelief or denial. They may find it difficult to understand why the person with OCD can't just stop acting out the ritual that so clearly makes everyone unhappy. A family member may say, "I was able to quit smoking; why can't you just stop all that checking?"

Families faced with the behaviours associated with OCD often experience complex and uncomfortable emotions. As the symptoms of OCD become more severe, the emotions that family members have may also become more intense. These emotions strain relationships and affect all aspects of family life. If allowed to escalate, the tension can become as hurtful as the disorder itself.

When your relative is first diagnosed

When someone in your family is diagnosed with OCD, you may feel many things. A diagnosis can bring a feeling of relief to finally know what the problem is. On the other hand, finding out that mental illness is the cause of your relative's worry and behaviour can make you feel sad. You may fear how the illness will affect the future—for your relative and for you. If you are a parent of a child or young adult who has been diagnosed with OCD, you may feel guilty and responsible. You may fear that you have done something to bring this on, even when professionals tell you that this is not the case. Not surprisingly, you may feel angry that OCD has disrupted family life.

It's normal to experience these varied and conflicting emotions. Understanding this, and learning to accept and manage your feelings, reduces the stress on you and helps you to provide more effective care for the person who is struggling with OCD.

Here are some tips that can help you to cope with the uncomfortable emotions that often arise when someone in your family has OCD. You can use these tips to help your relative recover.

How to relate to your family member with OCD

1. **Learn as much as you can about OCD and its treatment.** Being informed will help you to understand the illness and help your relative to make changes. See the list of recommended reading and websites beginning on page 53.

2. **View your relative's obsessive-compulsive behaviours as symptoms, not character flaws.** Remember that your relative is a person with a disorder, but is healthy and able in many other ways. Focus on them as a whole person.

3. **Do not allow OCD to take over family life.** As much as possible, keep stress low and family life normal.

4. **Do not participate in your relative's rituals.** If you have helped with rituals in the past, it may take time and practice to change this pattern. In order for people with OCD to make progress, family and friends must resist helping with ritual behaviours. Supporting the rituals, including reassurance rituals, hinders progress.

5. **Communicate positively, directly and clearly.** State what you want to happen, rather than criticizing your relative for past behaviours. Avoiding personal criticism can help your relative to feel accepted while he or she is making difficult changes.

6. **Keep calm.** Not losing your temper creates a good atmosphere.

7. **Remember that life is a marathon, not a sprint.** Progress is made in small steps. There are times when no progress is made at all. Applaud progress when times are good and provide encouragement when times are bad. Your support benefits your relative.

8. **Mix humour with caring.** Support doesn't always have to be serious. People with OCD know how absurd their fears are. They can often see the funny side of their symptoms, as long as the humour does not feel disrespectful. Family members say that humour can often help their relative to become more detached from symptoms.

9. **Know the signs that show your relative is struggling with his or her OCD.** Here are some of the signs noted by family members:
   - doing tasks over and over
   - having trouble completing a task

- arriving late because of repeatedly checking
- feeling too responsible for harm that may come to others
- constantly asking for reassurance
- saving and hoarding
- washing too much
- avoiding being with people
- avoiding certain places or activities
- becoming irritable when rituals are interfered with.

10. **Support your relative's medication and treatment program.**

11. **Don't forget that you are only human.** While you do your best to support your relative, you will sometimes find yourself participating in a ritual or giving reassurance. Try not to judge yourself when you fall into old routines, in the same way you try not to judge your relative. Just start again. No one is perfect.

12. **Take care of yourself.**
    - Keep your own support network.
    - Avoid becoming isolated.
    - Know what situations within your family are most stressful as you cope with you relative's OCD.
    - Develop interests outside the family.
    - Create a low-stress environment for yourself.
    - Take a little time each day just for you.

> *Mary's family was relieved when her OCD was finally diagnosed. Mary herself was relieved to discover there were treatments available. At first, she doubted the treatments could really help her, but she genuinely wanted to lead a more satisfying life and knew her problems made life difficult for the whole family. She made a firm commitment to follow through on the therapy recommendations.*

Her family recognized that they were going to need some help as well. They wanted to be able to support Mary. They attended support groups, read books about OCD and followed through on the recommendations. For the first time, they were able to openly discuss Mary's OCD as a problem for the whole family. With the support of her family, Mary was able to remain committed to her treatment program. Everyone benefited as family life began to improve.

Taking care of yourself

Caught up in concern and caring for the person who is ill, family members may not take proper care of themselves. They may give up their own activities and become isolated from their friends and colleagues. This may go on for some time before they realize they are emotionally and physically drained. The stress can lead to sleeping problems, exhaustion and constant irritability.

You need to know these signs of stress and look after your own physical and mental health. Recognizing your own limits and making time for yourself are keys to self-care. Make sure you have support from reliable friends and relatives. Mental illness is a hard thing for some people to grasp. You may want to confide only in people you know to be supportive.

Sometimes it is wise to get professional support. Join a self-help organization or support program for relatives of people with OCD. Such programs may be offered by a community mental health organization, clinic or local hospital.

Keep up your interests outside of the family and apart from your ill relative. Know and accept that sometimes you will feel negative about the situation. These feelings are normal and should not have to cause guilt.

Explaining OCD to children

Explaining OCD to children can be awkward and difficult. Parents may say nothing because they don't know how to explain it, or perhaps think that children couldn't understand. They may try to protect children from OCD and continue with family routines as if nothing were wrong.

It is difficult to maintain this strategy over time because the symptoms of OCD show up in behaviour. Children are very sensitive and intuitive. They notice when someone in the family has changed, or when tension surfaces. If the atmosphere in the family suggests that the subject should not be discussed, children will develop their own, often wrong, ideas.

Young children often see the world as revolving around themselves. This is especially true of children between three to seven years. If something happens that upsets people in the family, they may think it is their fault. For example, if someone fears contamination and becomes upset after a child touches a "contaminated" object, the child may assume he or she is the cause of the ill person's extreme behaviour.

To explain mental illness and OCD to children, it is important to tell them only as much as they are mature enough to understand. Toddlers and preschool children can understand simple, short sentences. These need to be worded in concrete language without much technical information. For example: "Sometimes daddy feels sick and it makes him upset." "When mommy is sick, touching the sink makes her upset."

Elementary-school children can process more information. They are able to understand the concept of OCD as an illness, but may be overwhelmed by details about therapies and medications. OCD could be explained to children of this age group like this: "OCD is a kind of illness that makes people worry a lot about germs and getting sick. Worrying so much makes them do things over and over again."

Teenagers are generally able to manage most information. They often need to talk about what they see and feel. They may ask about the genetics of OCD, or they may worry about the stigma of mental illness. Sharing information creates more dialogue.

When speaking to children, it is helpful to cover three main areas:

1. **The parent or family member behaves this way because he or she is sick.** It is important to tell children that the family member has a sickness called obsessive-compulsive disorder. OCD should be explained as an illness. You might explain it like this: "OCD is like chicken pox or a cold, except that rather than giving people spots or a runny nose, it makes them worry a lot, sometimes for no reason. This worry makes people with OCD check things over and over, or stay away from things that bother them, or collect stuff. Sometimes, they want people in their family to behave the same way. OCD takes a long time to get better. People with OCD need help from a doctor or therapist."

2. **Reassure the child that he or she did not make the parent or family member get this illness.** Children need to know they did not cause their loved one to develop the illness through something they did or did not do. People with OCD may become depressed as they struggle with their symptoms. Reassure children that they did not make their loved one sad.

3. **Reassure the child that adults in the family and other people
    such as doctors are trying to help the affected person.** Taking
    care of someone with OCD is an adult responsibility. It is not
    something children should have to worry about. Children
    need the well parent and other trusted adults to shield them
    from the effects of living with someone with OCD. Children
    should talk about what they see and feel with someone who
    knows how hard it is for their mother, father or relative to
    struggle with the symptoms. Many children are scared by
    the changes they see in their loved one. They miss the time
    spent with that person. Doing activities outside the home
    helps because it exposes children to other healthy relation-
    ships. As the ill parent recovers, slowly resuming family ac-
    tivities can help to mend the relationship between the child
    and the ill parent.

Both the ill parent and the well parent should talk with their
children about explaining the illness to people outside the family. Support from friends is important for everyone, but OCD can
be hard to explain and some families worry about the stigma of
mental illness. How open you and your children want to be is a
very individual choice.

Finally, some parents struggling with OCD may find that they are
less patient and more easily irritated. For them, the loud, messy,
chaotic play of children may be very hard to tolerate. Structured
routines ensure the ill parent has quiet, restful time, away
from situations that might trigger stress and conflict. You may
need to plan time for the children to play outside the home, or
arrange for the ill parent to rest for part of the day in a quiet
area of the house.

Once into recovery, it helps for the parent who was ill to explain his
or her behaviour to the children. The recovered parent may need

to plan some special times with the children. He or she may need to re-establish the relationship and reassure the children that he or she is now more available to them. In some instances, working with a therapist to formulate a plan can be very helpful.

Resources

SUGGESTED READING

Baer, L. (2012). *Getting Control: Overcoming Your Obsessions and Compulsions* (3rd ed.). New York: Plume.

Foa, E. & Wilson, R. (2001). *Stop Obsessing!: How to Overcome Your Obsessions and Compulsions.* New York: Bantam.

Hyman, B.M. & Pedrick, C. (2010). *The OCD Workbook: Your Guide to Breaking Free from Obsessive-Compulsive Disorder* (3rd ed). Oakland, CA: New Harbinger.

Landsman, K.J., Rupertus, K.M. & Pedrick, C. (2005). *Loving Someone with OCD: Help for You and Your Family.* Oakland, CA: New Harbinger.

Schwartz, J.M. (1996). *Brain Lock: Free Yourself from Obsessive-Compulsive Behaviour.* New York: Regan Books.

Steketee, G. & White, K. (1990). *When Once Is Not Enough: Help for Obsessive Compulsives.* Oakland, CA: New Harbinger.

INTERNET RESOURCES

Anxiety Disorders Association of America
www.adaa.org/understanding-anxiety/obsessive-compulsive-disorder-ocd

Canadian Institute for Obsessive Compulsive Disorders
www.ictoc.org

Canadian Mental Health Foundation
www.cmha.ca/mental_health/obsessive-compulsive-disorder

Canadian OCD Network
www.canadianocdnetwork.com

Frederick W. Thompson Anxiety Disorders Centre
www.sunnybrook.ca/thompsoncentre

National Institute of Mental Health
www.nimh.nih.gov/health/topics/obsessive-compulsive-disorder-ocd/index.shtml

Other guides in this series

Addiction

Anxiety Disorders

Bipolar Disorder

Borderline Personality Disorder

Cognitive-Behavioural Therapy

Concurrent Substance Use and Mental Health Disorders

Depression

Dual Diagnosis

First Episode Psychosis

The Forensic Mental Health System in Ontario

Schizophrenia

Women, Abuse and Trauma Therapy

Women and Psychosis

This publication may be available in other formats. For information about alternative formats or other camh publications, or to place an order, please contact camh Publications:

Toll-free: 1 800 661-1111
Toronto: 416 595-6059
E-mail: publications@camh.ca
Online store: http://store.camh.ca